Farming & Flourishing
on Sixty Acres

Steve Elzinga

Copyright © 2013 Steve Elzinga

I am very grateful to my editor, Keith Miller, without whom I would never have gotten this book to print. His comments and editing skills were invaluable to me. I'm also grateful for help from Caitlin Kreamer, Jim Brien (both employees), and my son, Jesse Elzinga, as well as my wife, Nancy Elzinga. All of them made helpful and positive comments, which encouraged me to pursue this endeavor!

Contents

Introduction..1
Chapter 1: Where to Buy Your Farm:
   Three Big Decisions......................................4
Chapter 2: Taking the Plunge............................10
Chapter 3: Growing Crops to Sell.......................21
Chapter 4: School Tours....................................25
Chapter 5: Entertainment..................................31
Chapter 6: Crop Diversification..........................41
Chapter 7: Observations about Retail Sales...........54
Chapter 8: Customer and Employee Relations.......65
Chapter 9: New Equipment
   and Capital Investments.............................70
Chapter 10: Customer Relations.........................74
Chapter 11: Conclusion....................................80

Introduction

I have a farm in Michigan: sixty-three acres of mostly apples, peaches, plums, and blueberries. For forty years it has been my passion and my work. Every year since 1977, I have kept files of receipts, invoices, correspondence, and notes on the crops. When the ceiling of my office began to sag from the weight of the files in the attic, I removed them to our garage at home, where my family hinted that it was time to burn them. I couldn't do it! The notes and memories from those files prompted this book.

Many of my customers and friends have told me of their desire to eat more locally grown fruits and vegetables. Some have even tried growing their own in their gardens. It is to these friends and to my own family that I dedicate this book and my experience of growing fruits.

This story began in 1977, after my wife Nancy and I had spent two and a half years in Kenya, East Africa. We were in Kenya as volunteers with Mennonite Central Committee (MCC)—a mission and service organization of the Mennonite Church. MCC seconded me to the Ministry of Agriculture and Nancy to the Ministry of Gender, Children, and Social Development. We lived and worked in the town of Garissa, in a remote area of Kenya's Northeastern Province. I worked with local farmers developing some cash crops and exploring simple ways to irrigate small plots along the Tana River. Nancy initially taught at a local high school and later worked as a social worker. This experience as volunteers changed our lives and altered my career.

With degrees in economics, my choices for employment were mostly large corporations, banks, or the government. After working with small farmers and small-scale farming in the tropics, none of those prospects interested me.

I grew up six miles from a family apple orchard. My great-grandfather, Hemka (Henry) Elzinga, had purchased the orchard in northern Michigan in the late 1890s. It remained in our extended family for more than a hundred years. My second cousin, John Elzinga, was the last owner of this orchard and farm—it was sold in 2001. My uncle, Arthur Elzinga, and aunt, Connie Raymer, also owned orchards in Michigan. Though I never lived or worked on these farms, they were a part of our family history. Hence, it seemed quite natural to buy and learn to operate an orchard.

Today, forty years later, I look back with awe and humility, recognizing that we have survived and prospered on this farm. Though we have endured a number of calamities, including drought, floods, hail, and killing frosts, I have also experienced great joy in tending and harvesting our fruits.

We have been remarkably fortunate to have a crop of apples nearly every year. Even when other areas of our state have suffered from late spring frosts or winter temperature extremes, we have escaped with abundant harvests. And, though our peach trees suffered during the winters of 2014 and 2015, we had twenty years of excellent peach harvests. Beautiful late September and October weekends will bring up to ten thousand customers. Many second-generation families now make an annual outing to our farm.

As I write down as accurately as possible my experiences on the farm, I hope it may have some historical interest, as well as be of some use to those who wish to start their own orchard or farm-related enterprise.

Chapter 1
Where to Buy Your Farm: Three Big Decisions

I love Washington, New York, San Francisco, Boston, London, and Nairobi. My family and I often visit these cities, where we enjoy the theater, the parks, the museums, and just being a part of the masses on a crowded sidewalk on a Sunday afternoon. But I hate working in cities. Perhaps people lose their special friendliness because we no longer have to ask the obvious after we move there. Perhaps the museums are too close to enjoy. Perhaps the theater becomes too late and the train ride too monotonous.

You might also be tired of city life. Perhaps you too want to go to Vermont, northern Michigan, northern California, southern Ohio, western Texas, or upstate New York. You want to go where the land is relatively inexpensive and where you can use your home equity to start a new life growing and selling produce. You might go back to the city occasionally. But mostly you just want the quiet beauty of the forest and the sweet smell of spring flowers.

Forget it! It won't work. Even if you have a pocket full of cash, a trust account to back you up, and a Learjet to get you out, don't go! At least, not if you want to seriously farm. You need the city. You need the people. You need to be close to them. That should be your first and most important decision. Find that bucolic, wonderful farm with all its attractions, but make sure it's a stone's throw from the last suburb of a large city.

When, after returning from Kenya, I told my relatives about my desire to raise apples and other fruits, their first reaction was to probe my sanity. Their second was to advise me to go as far from the orchard country and as close to the city as possible. They were right. My orchard is the only commercial-size facility in our county between Detroit and Toledo. We have about 2 million people within an hour's drive. Nearby, we also have several small cities promoting "tailgate farmers' markets," an extremely important part of our business, as you will see.

The simple facts are these:

1. If you are going to grow fruits and vegetables on relatively small acreage (a hundred acres or less) and you are serious about making money, you need to sell 90 percent or more of it directly to the end user—the customer. That customer must be close to you. The best and most obvious sale is right on your

premises. Preferably, a portion of your acreage will border on a major highway. You may be slightly more remote, but only if you have a large population nearby that is able to find you. Don't go to that mountain retreat or far-off prairie to fulfill your dream. It will become a nightmare.

2. Andrew Tobias, in *The Only Investment Guide You'll Ever Need*, says—about buying real estate, stock, or anything else—that one should buy low and sell high. Sounds great, looks good, and makes sense. Unfortunately, it's just what most of us don't do most of the time. But with your land investment, you're going to have to work at it. The deals are out there. You can't compete with the real-estate barons anticipating a shopping mall just beyond the last shopping mall. You will have to go beyond them. But, remember, don't go too far!

I recently went to a seminar attended by farm marketers. One marketer related how he is being "pushed" into direct retail sales by city folks. His orchard and market are located in West Virginia, close to the Maryland border. He is feeling the rising tide of population from Washington, D.C., northern Virginia, and Frederick County, Maryland. He is in an enviable position: his state has relatively low taxes, yet he is close to major population centers across the border. I wanted to tell him to develop a five-year plan to phase out his wholesale business and go after the retail customers across the border. Opportunities like his are tremendously exciting and can provide incredible growth.

3. Recognize the farm for what it is to the city people. They love the farm. Many people have a grandpa and grandma, uncle and aunt, or distant cousin who has owned a farm. They remember visiting it as children, and the positive experiences that came along with it. Now they want their children to have the same feeling.

At our orchard we want you to see and feel it all. You can watch the apple grader clean and sort our fruit. You can watch the cider ooze from the stained cloths. You can pet our goats, turkeys, and ponies, and you can walk into the refrigerator where we store the fruit for the winter. It's a place to come with your family, reminisce about the old days, have a picnic, take a walk, and let the dog and kids roam. We give hayrides and pony rides. Both young and old love these activities. We have craft shows, antique car shows, pumpkin festivals, and apple festivals. We have a gift shop. You can pick your own blueberries, peaches, apples, and pumpkins. On a fall weekend, if you want to do something unusual with your out-of-town guests, we have the place for you. Does your company want to host an unusual party? We will provide a hayride, bonfire site, donuts, cider, and hot dogs.

When you buy that land, and when you gather the necessary equipment to make it work for you, you have something immensely interesting to most people. So sell it to them! Oh, yes, you will want to grow some fruit; you will want to have the equipment and facilities to legitimize you as a bona fide producer. But never forget that you are interesting. And the essence of your survival is not in the production of your fruits and vegetables; it is in capitalizing on the interest that others have in your production of fruit and vegetables. Charge them to see you do it.

Have you ever visited the Napa Valley wineries in California? The processing of grapes into wine has long since been removed from the barns and vats that occupy the old estates, and I expect the production of grapes will soon disappear as well. Nevertheless, the farms still have the feel, the smell—the sense that something old and natural, good and wholesome was made there. The owners of the vineyard (the corporation) have captured us. Do you think the wine-tasting and production-facility tours are there to supplement the grape-growing business? No, the grape-growing is a mere sideshow to the revenues generated from the tremendously popular wine-tasting tour. If you decide to invest in a mini-farm, you must have that concept in mind.

The revenues from our "extracurricular" activities, including hay and pony rides, inflatables, company picnics, birthday parties and booth rentals for crafters, have eclipsed the income from our fruit over the last decade. For example, on a busy fall weekend we will take up to two thousand customers on a hayride into the orchard. At $5 per ticket, the hayrides alone will generate $10,000 in revenues. Pick-your-own-fruit revenues, while still important, seldom exceed $5,000 even on busy weekends.

Chapter 2
Taking the Plunge

I don't know all the best ways to creatively finance your purchase. I'll leave that to the "experts." I will simply share how I did it, and let you pick out any details that may be helpful.

I discovered our farm and orchard in a newspaper advertisement in March, 1977. The orchard met my criteria of being close to a major metropolitan area with very few orchards nearby. It was already operating as a farm with a seasonal market for retail sales. The owner had already made the transition from a traditional production-oriented wholesale apple orchard to a "pick-your-own" retail establishment. Hence, we already had a customer base to begin to cultivate. The price was $130,000, which included sixty-two acres of tillable ground and buildings in various stages of disrepair, a barn converted into a farm market, a cider mill, a pole barn, a cold-storage building, and a couple of small outbuildings. There was no home. I told the realtor that I wanted it but had absolutely no money for a down payment. In order to buy the orchard, I would need to find a suitable partner.

I found a partner, who was the president of a local bank, and we paid the owner $34,000 down, and asked him to carry the balance of $96,000 for one year at 9 percent with interest paid monthly. I raised the $17,500 for my share of the down payment from my parents and in-laws. After one year, largely on the financial strength of my partner, we financed $96,000 with a local commercial bank. The property was amortized for twelve and a half years, requiring an annual payment of $8,000, due as follows: $2,000 Sept. 1, $2,000 Oct. 1, $2,000 Nov. 1, and $2,000 Dec. 1. Interest was paid monthly on the remaining balance.

When interest rates soared to 18 percent in 1981, and our local bank reneged on our loan cap, we refinanced with Greenstone Farm Credit Services (now Greenstone Credit Services). The loan, at $116,000, was amortized over twenty years with one payment of principal and interest paid annually, $16,500. In 1985, I purchased my partner's shares for $135,000. I paid him $50,000 cash (largely from money I borrowed from family and friends) and he held a note for $85,000. The payment terms were 11 percent annual interest with one payment annually of $9,350 every October.

In 1989, I completed this transaction by paying my partner with a loan from the Farmers Home Administration, a federal government agency that creates loans, primarily for farmers. The note was for $85,000, amortized over thirty years at 5 percent interest. I asked and qualified for a low-interest status, which we'll look at more closely in a moment.

Here are a few observations on the above:

Partners

They can be a lot of trouble. But in my case, at least initially, I could not have made it alone. Our arrangement worked fine. I did all the work, was paid a salary (sub-poverty level), and kept the place going. My partner provided the financial muscle to get the necessary loans. We had problems and differences. But we also had fun and enjoyed the unique camaraderie that one has when making joint decisions about the business. As with all relationships, ours changed, and we eventually decided to split up. It was the right decision.

Debt

Initially, I carried a high debt level. In 1989 I had about $220,000 in long-term mortgages: $100,000 in original loans with the Greenstone Credit Service, a $35,000 second mortgage taken out for building renovation, and $85,000 from buying out my partner. I had roughly another $50,000 in short-term loans on new equipment purchased. This kind of debt on sixty acres of land and a few buildings frightened many people. But I also had an income of about $325,000 a year, with roughly $100,000 available for debt services. In other words, if you added my net income, my interest expense, and then depreciation expense, you would arrive at a figure that banks consider available to service debt. If you ever need to deal with a banker, you will learn all about cash flows. Over the years, our debt-to-income ratio has decreased significantly. This is reflected in the graph on the next page, with decreasing interest over the years 1986–2015.

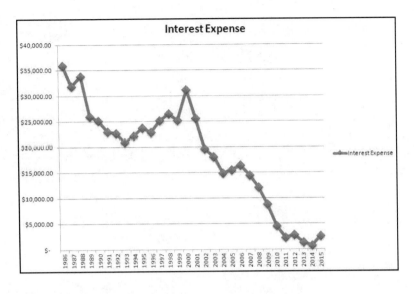

1986- $35,888.07	1987- $31,842.32	1988- $33,807.00
1989- $25,971.00	1990- $25,209.00	1991- $23,039.00
1992- $22,714.00	1993- $20,928.00	1994- $22,205.00
1995- $23,772.00	1996- $22,882.00	1997- $25,218.00
1998- $26,494.00	1999- $25,200.00	2000- $31,125.00
2001- $25,604.00	2002- $19,601.00	2003- $18,066.00
2004- $14,903.00	2005- $15,474.00	2006- $16,455.00
2007- $14,472.00	2008- $12,120.00	2009- $8,803.00
2010- $4,561.00	2011- $2,296.00	2012- $2,783.00
2013- $1,371.00	2014- $764.00	2015- $2,600.00

Living with debt

How much debt is too much? You must be careful here, because life can become extremely unpleasant if you can't meet your obligations. On the farm, you should anticipate at least 25 percent more cost and 10 percent less income than you conservatively projected. In other words, draw up a conservative projection of expenses and income for your first year and then begin to slash income and increase expenses. If, after this, you still see room to "service the debt," you can at least continue to consider it.

Other income

Don't completely give up other sources of income. If you are married, one of you should be working another job. Don't rely on the farm as your total source of income initially. My wife, Nancy, is a social worker at a local hospital. While she has been supportive of me and the farm, she has pursued her own career. Her income and health insurance proved essential during the "lean" years at the orchard.

Farm Credit Services

Rough times on the farm in the 1980s forced this bank to reevaluate all its lending policies. Don't expect any deals from the Greenstone Credit Services. The interest rate doesn't rise as fast as other banks during upward cycles, but neither does it drop as fast during downward cycles. The reason for this is that most of the funding for these banks comes from the bond market. In short, you will find better amortization schedules and more flexible payment plans (you can pay once a year, after the harvest season). Also, they will not fall off their caster chair when you tell them you want to farm for a living. You must be prepared to provide the same detailed financial statement, projection, and payback ability with the Greenstone as you would with any other commercial lending institution.

Farmers Home Administration

Under the aegis of the Department of Agriculture, the FmHA is a funding agency for farmers who are having difficulties finding funding elsewhere. There are several offices in most states, and they can be helpful. There are three criteria for applying for funding with the FmHA: 1) you have to have been rejected by at least two commercial banks (this is usually not a problem—see Tobias!); 2) you have to be located in a rural area, outside city limits; and 3) you need patience.

I have found the Farmers Home Administration staff honest and professional. Yes, you will deal with seemingly unnecessary paperwork, but it is not insurmountable. The problem is availability of funds. Traditionally, the FmHA has funded both farm ownership and farm operation. Due to recent budget cuts, the FmHA has decided to eliminate most of its real estate lending, continuing primarily as a backup for farmers who need money to operate. Thus, you will find it much easier to obtain funds to operate rather than to buy a farm. In spite of this, as described above, I received an ownership loan to buy out my partner at very favorable rates. But it took three years of prodding. Don't give up. It will take some effort to obtain any kind of government financing but it is worth it.

The FmHA also has a loan guarantee program. They will, under this program, guarantee your loan with a commercial bank or FCS bank up to 90 percent of its face value. Most commercial banks don't participate under this program, but if you can find one that does, it's an effective tool to help you and your lender.

Business structure

Concerning type of business, there are several alternatives, including sole proprietorship, partnership, and corporation. You want to be careful in making this decision because it will influence your taxes, and this is important. In this section, I'll outline how I did it.

Charles J. Givens, in *Wealth Without Risk*, states that "the biggest lifetime expense you'll ever encounter is neither a home nor a college education, but income taxes" (p. 125). Reducing your tax liability is a good step toward capturing some of it. My first few years in business I paid no taxes and, in fact, received back all withheld taxes from my wife's salary. How did I do it? I chose the Chapter S Corporation for my business. Under this arrangement, your business is a full-fledged corporation, but all income or losses from the business flow through you and your partner's individual tax returns. Because our farm had an orchard and several buildings with equipment, we had large depreciation expenses (fruit trees are depreciable assets). And, although we made some money after expenses in our first years, when I added in the depreciation expense, we showed several years of losses, which I carried to my individual return. (For more on depreciation expenses, see Donald Trump's informative discussion in *The Art of a Deal*, p. 143.) You can, of course, choose to be an individual proprietor in which case you would use a schedule "C" on your individual 1040. The schedule "C" allows you to deduct expenses and depreciation from your income and any gain or loss will transfer directly to your 1040, much the same as filing as an "S" corporation.

We discovered, however, that by choosing the "S" as the chapter's corporation, we became eligible for some added deductions. For example, we claimed a domestic production credit (a credit for producing a product in the USA). This credit, not available to individual filers, saved us several hundred dollars annually on our taxes.

Of course there are limits on the losses you can carry, along with numerous technicalities, which appear just when you believe you have the answers.

But you must make the decision wisely, based on your tax considerations. For this, you must consult several tax accountants. Don't stop asking questions and don't take the advice of just one expert. This will be, next to your farm's location, your most important decision. See the depreciation graph on the next page for the years 1986–2015.

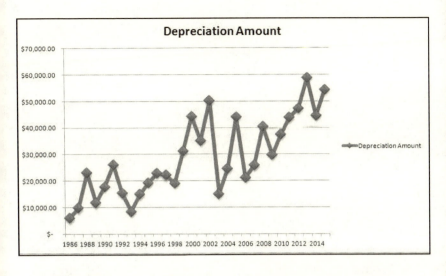

1986- $5,889.27	1987- $9,787.00	1988- $22,997.00
1989- $11,713.00	1990- $17,815.00	1991- $26,127.00
1992- $15,362.00	1993- $8,429.00	1994- $14,947.00
1995- $19,293.00	1996- $22,863.00	1997- $22,176.00
1998- $19,043.00	1999- $31,152.00	2000- $44,271.00
2001- $35,152.00	2002- $50,219.00	2003- $15,061.00
2004- $24,652.00	2005- $44,092.00	2006- $21,183.00
2007- $25,839.00	2008- $40,443.00	2009- $29,756.00
2010- $37,532.00	2011- $43,758.00	2012- $47,167.00
2013- $58,815.00	2014- $44,471.00	2015- $54,382.00

Chapter 3
Growing Crops to Sell

If you've never been much for gardening and you don't care about soil, hoes, and weeds, let alone thriving crops, then you should not start this venture. Don't fret if you don't like equipment (I don't) and are not mechanically inclined (I'm not). You can master these deficiencies. But if your spirit is not into trees, plants, and the great wonder of growing, don't do this.

I will often return to the farm on a warm summer night after dinner to hoe a row or two of pumpkins. I do it because I want to. For me there is no greater joy than being a part of the growing environment—weeding, pruning, and feeding my plants. Please understand that I love the theater, a good baseball game on a summer evening, or a night at the pool with my family. But, if I had to choose one activity, I would return to the farm and pull weeds. And believe me, you will have to pull weeds!

There will be constant minor crises: the beetles are eating the emerging pumpkin plants, the tentiform leafminer is hatching in the apple orchard, there are thistles growing in the raspberries, weeds have over taken the new apricot trees . . .

Occasionally there will be a major crisis. On August 4, 1988, after surviving a drought for three months, we had a hailstorm. It was catastrophic. We were going to pick our peaches the next day, and our apples were just beginning to get to size. In thirty seconds every fruit in our orchard had been injured or destroyed. I cried. But we mustered every force we had and we survived. We expanded our school tour program (more on this later). We bought peaches and apples elsewhere. We wrote a letter to every customer in our mailing list explaining what had happened. Fortunately, we also carried hail insurance.

And that was just the first of our crises. In 1989 we had about twenty inches of rain in six weeks during our planting season. Our pumpkins and winter squash had to be replanted twice. They never did ripen satisfactorily. That crisis, mild though it was compared to 1988, cost us several thousand dollars and many customers in October. In the nineties we survived a chemical scare (Alar) and *E. coli* bacteria discovered in unpasteurized cider in a California orchard. In 1994 an extremely cold winter killed every peach bud and we had no crop. In 2001 it rained nearly every day in October, the month that generates nearly half our income. From 2008 through 2015, the participants in our school field trip program dwindled from a high of 18,000 to 6,000 (more on this later).

In 2014 and 2015 winter temperatures plunged to record lows. We recorded −18 F degrees on two or three nights in both years. Not only did the peach buds freeze; over 90 percent of all our trees died. We bulldozed nearly a thousand trees in the spring of 2015, basically removing us from the peach business.

In spite of these setbacks, our income climbed. We reached $500,000 in 2002, $600,000 in 2007, $650,000 in 2014. (See p. 30 for total sales) While these increases are gradual, the reduction of interest expense gave our net income a huge boost in 2014 and 2015. (Note: net income is on p. 62 and interest expense on p. 14).

How was I able to handle these failures and survive? Diversification into areas that are less dependent on weather for income generation was one answer for us. We have branched out into three main areas: 1) school field trips and weekend hayrides, 2) entertainment, and 3) crop diversification. For example, in 1985, I informally surveyed customers who were visiting our orchard and asked how they knew about us. Since we spend about 3 percent of our total revenue on advertising, I am always curious to see what is working. I was surprised to learn roughly 70 percent came because their son or daughter had visited us on a school field trip. For several years I had resisted doing school field trips. We are busy harvesting, grading, and selling our fruit in the fall. Giving young children a tour of our facility and explaining the process of growing apples and making cider seemed an unnecessary and annoying interference until I took this survey. I realized that giving tours of our facility to busloads of school kids may be the best advertising we have. And instead of paying, we are being paid to advertise! The next three chapters highlight the three areas of diversification.

Chapter 4
School Tours

In 1986 I decided to promote our field trip program. I hired two women to send letters to our local school districts outlining what we do and what we can offer. We drew about 5,000 children the first year, and the numbers grew in subsequent years. In 1989 we reached 13,000 school children; in 1996, 22,000; and in 2001, 25,000, including our weekend hayrides. In 1989 we charged $2 per participant for our tour; in 2015 we charged $8.

The tours follow this pattern: The children are led from arriving buses and directed toward the animal center, where they may pet the goats and feed the chickens. They are then helped onto hay wagons for a tour of the orchard, where they learn how the trees are pollinated, how the apples grow, and how we care for the orchard. Each child picks three apples. They then return to the main facility, where they observe the functioning of the apple grader, the cold storage room, and the cider press. At the end of the tour, we serve each participant a glass of cider and a donut. As they leave, they choose a small pie pumpkin from a bin. What does the school tour program mean to us? It has benefited our operation in four significant ways.

First, it produces income even when the crop is below standard. For example, the children picked our hail-damaged fruit in 1988 even though we could not use it for fresh market produce. The fruit was fine, but bruised where the hail had hit it. Since most of the rationale for these field trips is to provide an outdoor educational and recreational activity, the process of picking and learning are more important than the quality of the fruit.

Our 1989 records show that on a day when we brought three hundred children through the facility we generated about $900. Each participant spent an average of $1 in addition to the $2 fee. Most kids have some change, and mothers and chaperones can't resist buying donuts, cider, and apple products. This, of course, is in addition to the sales to regular customers throughout the day. In 2012 we ran an average of three to four hundred participants per day in October, at $8 each. We discovered that each participant spends an average of $12 ($8 for the field trip and $4 on miscellaneous items from our store). Thus, our daily gross sales are $4,800 before considering our regular customers for that day.

Second, our tour program benefits our operation by effectively advertising through children. If children have a wonderful time, parents will have a wonderful time. And if children like your place, parents will like your place—you can depend on it. McDonald's Corporation spent millions to equip their franchises with children's play areas. They know the benefits of advertising through children. Children who visit our operation receive drawstring plastic bags to put their apples in. The bag displays our name, address, phone number, and other information about the orchard.

Third, the tours benefit our business by creating excitement even on dull rainy days. Any merchandiser will tell you how important traffic flow is to your sales volume. When stores are filled with shoppers, a shortage psychology often develops. Shoppers begin to believe that if they don't buy the object that interests them, someone else surely will the moment they lay it down. It happens every year in the big chain stores on prime shopping days before Christmas. Children filling up our store during normally slow weekdays creates the same effect, and sales climb.

Finally, tours provide a clear path toward increased revenue. All primary school teachers want good, clean, educational tours for their classes. They especially desire a well-organized tour that provides hands-on experience, such as picking apples and pumpkins.

As mentioned earlier, we witnessed a steady decline in school field trip participation from 2007 through 2015. There were two reasons for this: First, schools, both public and private, have reduced funding for field trips and extracurricular activities. Many teachers who had brought their students annually can no longer finance the bus transportation and trip expense. Second, we have competition. Several small pumpkin farms and corn-maze operations offer similar field trips. Museums, parks, and special exhibits such as butterfly houses offer alternative and less-expensive field trips.

How did we meet this challenge? Here are three ways:

We added more tractors and wagons for our weekend hayrides. Although we charge less ($4) for the weekend ride, we are getting more participants who enjoy a hayride to the orchard with their family. We do not do a full field trip on these weekend rides. Participants are given a half-hour scenic ride to the orchard, where they can pick two apples. On a busy September or October weekend, we average eight hundred to a thousand participants. We operate seven wagons carrying thirty people each during the peak demand between two and four on Saturday and Sunday afternoons.

Company picnics have also helped offset income losses from the school field trips. We offer two large pole buildings (30' x 80') for company outings on our September and October weekends. The buildings rent for $250, and we offer a discount on activities, including the pony, hayrides, corn maze, inflatables, and you-pick fruit.

Finally, we have expanded our area for crafters who come and set up their various wares for sale. On most weekends we have thirty to fifty crafters who pay a nominal fee of $20 per day or $30 per weekend. Although the rental income is not huge, the excitement generated by the large displays of homemade crafts is an added attraction for our customers.

Although we miss the daily influx of school field trip participants, our total gross income grew to a near-record level in 2014. The expanded activities mentioned above contributed significantly to the increase in income. See total sales on the next page from the years 1986–2015.

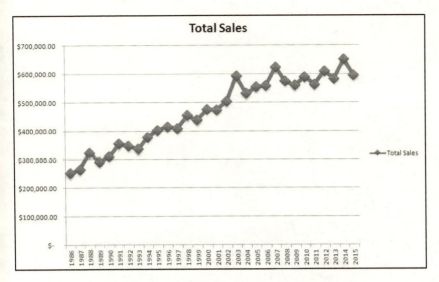

1986- $251,558.16   1987- $265,308.10   1988- $323,782.00

1989- $291,681.00   1990- $311,024.00   1991- $354,846.00

1992- $347,613.00   1993- $337,097.00   1994- $378,134.00

1995- $402,813.00   1996- $415,065.00   1997- $408,586.00

1998- $454,420.00   1999- $438,102.00   2000- $475,336.00

2001- $473,045.00   2002- $503,256.00   2003- $591,902.00

2004- $531,243.00   2005- $552,737.00   2006- $558,094.00

2007- $622,831.00   2008- $574,000.00   2009- $558,934.00

2010- $588,299.00   2011- $561,993.00   2012- $608,656.00

2013- $582,745.00   2014- $650,698.00   2015- 594,709.00

Chapter 5
Entertainment

In 1989, while planning for the next seven fall weekends, I called a friend who was in the local classic-car club. I asked him to announce at the next meeting that, if their members would drive their cars to our orchard on a Sunday afternoon and display them for three hours (from 1 p.m. to 4 p.m.), I would give each driver a gallon of cider and a dozen donuts. My friend announced this and placed a two-line ad in the Sunday paper under antique/classic cars outlining my plan. He called and said we would probably get eight to ten cars for the first-time effort. In fact, we were overwhelmed: sixty cars showed up and we had the biggest revenue day in our history. It was even larger than our apple and pumpkin festival days!

We continued this annual car-show tradition for over twenty years. In 2001 and 2002 we reached five hundred cars! But we discovered that we can most efficiently accommodate about two hundred cars while still providing adequate parking for the other customers. Finally, in 2012, we discontinued the annual car show as we could not accommodate all the cars with our regular customers.

The car-show weekend was just one of seven fall weekend events, beginning the second weekend of September. The car show was usually the same weekend as the Apple Festival described below.

Weekend 1—Apple Festival
(Second weekend in September)

We offer chicken and pork BBQ, entertainment (live bands), pony and hayrides, and you-pick apples and peaches. We also serve homemade baked goods, donuts, and cider. We plan the weekend in early September to maximize revenues on a weekend that would not normally be very busy. Early to mid-September is still relatively warm at our location and customers are not yet in "fall apple" mode. Hence, these special events and food offerings attract customers who may otherwise be enjoying end-of-summer activities.

Weekend 2—Kids' Weekend 1
(Third weekend in September)

While this weekend includes most of the same items as the Apple Festival, including the baked goods, cider making, pony and hayrides, and apple picking, we also add special shows for children. These include a clown, face painting, inflatables, and balloon characters. It is very popular, and this weekend usually kicks off the big crowds, attracting several thousand customers both Saturday and Sunday. It also helps establish a pattern for us to follow for the remaining five weekends. We know how to handle the parking of several hundred cars, we have learned how to control the inventory, the staff members understand their roles, and we have worked through the usual problems that accompany handling large crowds.

Weekend 3—Pumpkin Festival
(Final weekend in September or first weekend of October)

This is a big weekend for us as we begin our pumpkin season. Although it is early for purchasing pumpkins (though a surprising number do buy this early), we offer a huge display of pumpkins. When the time comes, many customers will return for the pumpkins.

This weekend features the same events as the previous weekends. But we are now also booking parties for companies and groups. We erected a pole building, which groups can rent for a nominal fee. They can also purchase tickets for pony rides, hayrides, and inflatables at a reduced fee. In addition, we rent out space to crafters, who bring their own tents and tables and their crafts to sell. The fee is a modest $20 per day or $30 per weekend. While this is not a huge money-maker for us, it is an added attraction for customers. On many weekends we have twenty-five to thirty craft booths set up.

The Pumpkin Festival weekend introduces October, our busiest month of the season. Our total revenue for October 2011 was $280,000 out of a total of $565,000 for the year. In 2014 the October revenues were $271,232, and $650,698 for the year; in 2015, $281,049 and $598,865, respectively. The pumpkin weekend and the following two weekends in October also make the largest contribution to the corporate savings. We usually set a goal to save $150,000–175,000 per year. These funds are used during the "off" season from December to July to fund operations and improvements. Roughly two-thirds of the savings, or $100,000, must be recorded during this pumpkin weekend and the following two weekends.

Weekend 4—Harvest Festival
(First full weekend in October)

Harvest Festival weekend includes all the activities mentioned above. In addition, we often include a special afternoon on Saturday or Sunday featuring a local dance studio or singing club. I love to host these groups, which feature young students dancing or singing. The parents, grandparents, and other family members come to watch the performance and, of course, become customers. I've included a Saturday afternoon picture of an estimated crowd of five hundred watching a local dance group perform (see p. 40). This crowd translates into high cider and donut sales after the performance!

Weekend 5—Kids' Weekend 2
(Second weekend in October)

This is the biggest of them all (except if it rains, as it did in 2011). It is prime season for cider and donuts, as well as pumpkin and apple picking. Saturday and Sunday we have a magic show as we do during Kids' Weekend 1. But we also have a costume contest for children ages one to ten, with judging on Sunday at 3 p.m. We have as many as a hundred participants, and this has become a very special day for the kids, as well as their families and friends. I've hired a local businessman as MC. He wears an exotic Halloween costume as he talks with the parents and children. We take the time to introduce all the participants.

If this day is sunny, it is without question the busiest day of the year for us. When we have free entertainment, we charge $1 for parking on all weekends from noon to five p.m., and we have parked up to 1,800 cars. We give each car a $1 coupon. In previous years, this could be redeemed at the you-pick booths or ticket windows for pony and hayrides. However, this policy generated the only complaints I received during the season by those who came merely to get cider and donuts and couldn't redeem the coupon in our main store. I had justified this $1 fee to pay for the eight to ten people I have directing traffic and maintaining order, but I made the decision in 2012 to allow the $1 coupon to be used anywhere on the premises. So now the customer who comes in for only cider and donuts can also get credit with the $1 coupon. I compensated for this loss of income by raising the price of donuts—our most popular product and the one product least likely to be affected by a price increase.

The Kids' Weekend 2 represents the culmination of hard work and a long season. While we still have two important fall weekends following this one, nothing can compare to the volume of customers and sales on this middle weekend in October.

Weekends 6 and 7
(Third and fourth weekends in October)

On the last weekends in October we continue with the entertainment of the earlier weekends, while recognizing that the weather can alter plans. The emphasis is on pumpkin sales and cider making. The final two Sundays can be extremely busy if weather permits. In 2009, the third Sunday of the month, on a spectacular fall day, we had one of the largest revenue days in our history: over $30,000 for an afternoon.

As might be expected, these final weekends in October are the biggest pumpkin days. I've learned to bolster our pumpkin inventory by buying a couple of semi-loads in addition to what we grow, to meet the demand and to demonstrate that we have a huge inventory.

The competition for selling pumpkins is keen. Many smaller farms and produce markets sell pumpkins, cider, gourds, and other fall produce. It is important to provide some entertainment and other inducements to bring customers to the farm. As described in Chapter 6, no farm market or enterprise should be without pumpkins. It is a lucrative product, and the bigger and bolder the display the better!

Entrance sign to Erie Orchards and Cider Mill.

Employees Sarah Collier and Mike and Val Mitchell (managers) observing full bloom in the apple trees.

Steve working in the peach orchard at full bloom.

Crafters selling their crafts on the orchard grounds on a fall weekend.

Large crowds watching a local dance company perform at the orchard.

Our inflatables—part of the weekend entertainment for children.

Chapter 6
Crop Diversification

While I now believe that crops are less important to our overall revenues than entertainment, it is still important to maintain the image of a growing, working orchard with the option to pick your own fruit.

The last two decades have seen rapid movement away from single-breadwinner families in which Dad works and Mom cans food all summer. When I was growing up in the fifties and sixties, my mother, I believe, felt most satisfied when the basement pantry was filled with canned peaches, pears, green beans, beets, and other fruits and vegetables grown in the garden or nearby orchards. She labored on those hot August and September days to lay up food for the family during the winter (or for when the Cold War turned hot!). Mother continued a long tradition. Her mother and grandmother had done the same for their families.

However, that paradigm has shifted drastically. These days, both spouses work outside the home and the produce section of the grocery store offers every possible fruit and vegetable all year long. The desire, ability, and need to work in the kitchen in mid-August is gone . . .

This presents a problem for those of us in the production and retail sale of fruits and vegetables. How are we going to sell a bumper crop of peaches and blueberries when no one wants to buy large quantities? How can we expect to sell 15,000 bushels of apples from twenty-five acres of apple trees when the most common sale to a family is half a peck (an eighth of a bushel)? The answer is twofold for us: 1) we have attracted many more customers through entertainment, and hence more people to buy those half pecks; and 2) we have reduced the acreage of some of our fruit to equalize the supply with our demand.

This is how I see the future of our main crop:

Apples

We have reduced the acreage from roughly forty acres to twenty-five. We now buy up to a quarter of the apples we sell. This includes buying varieties that may be short for the year and buying popular varieties that we don't grow, such as Gala, Fuji, and Honeycrisp. The apples we grow are primarily the older traditional varieties of our area, including McIntosh, Red and Golden Delicious, Jonathan, Ida Red, Granny Smith, and Jonagold. We also have some old-fashioned varieties such as Northern Spy and Winesap. These varieties are unattractive but possess other wonderful qualities. They are great for pies, they store well, and they cannot be found in supermarkets. If you plant apple trees, I recommend that you stay with the varieties that are traditional in your region. You may want to try some of the newer varieties, but don't forget about the old standbys. (We have planted more Honeycrisp apples in 2014–15.)

I will not dwell on the details of planting apple trees, but my most successful block of apple trees consists of five varieties on a dwarf root stock of M7. The trees are about seven to eight feet tall full-grown and consistently produce good fruit. The many varieties provide excellent cross-pollination and this tree size makes for easy picking and pruning. This block of about a thousand trees sits on eight acres. I have removed three rows to make it easier to pull the hay wagon through this block for school tours. When planting, leave every fifth or sixth row unplanted so your wagons can pass through. My spacing for the trees in this block was 12' x 18', with eighteen feet being the distance between rows.

What is the future for apples? We will plant fewer trees and concentrate on areas described below. We are doing this for three reasons.

First, apples can be readily purchased at reasonable rates in most parts of the country. You can resell them in your retail market at a profit and without the effort of growing them.

Second, apple trees, while hardy, are highly susceptible to disease and insects. If most people were fully aware of the number and amount of chemicals sprayed onto apples in large commercial orchards, they would not eat them. We have tried to limit the use of chemicals by monitoring our insect populations and spraying only when necessary. Nevertheless, we do have to spray. We have subscribed to an integrated pest management program (IPM), in which a scout monitors our orchard for insects and diseases. We have been able to reduce the chemical spraying by 50 percent as a result. This is not only an environmental advantage but also economic. Each spray costs between $500 and $1,000, depending on chemicals needed. Jenny Caroen, our scout, provides valuable assistance not only in identifying pest and diseases, but also in recommending which chemical is most effective and least toxic to humans and the environment.

We seek to avoid systemic chemicals (those absorbed into the tree through the leaves) and use only surface and biodegradable chemicals.

I recommend hiring a scout to monitor your crops. But remember to find one knowledgeable about the chemicals needed to control pests and diseases. Often scouts are very effective in identifying diseases and insects, but they lack knowledge of chemical control. To win the battle of diseases and insects, you have to know both.

If you are planning to raise apples organically, I applaud you, but it will be a formidable task. We have tried. But controlling scab, mites, codling moths, and other disease-producing pests is almost impossible without some chemical control.

Finally, apple trees need to be pruned—a difficult and time-consuming task. To keep the trees properly trained for maximum production and quality, you should prune annually. Most large orchards don't get to each block of trees every year, but there is a price to pay for this: when you do prune, you will have larger cuts and more unwieldy branches. All fruit trees need pruning, but apples are the most demanding.

I recommend planting an apple orchard of not more than fifteen acres to accommodate school groups and pick-your-own customers. This size will give the perception of a big orchard, but you will be able to handle the spraying, pruning, and other care without a huge effort.

Peaches

Peaches are difficult to grow and maintain at our latitude. Severe winters with frequent and sudden temperature changes cause the fast-growing peach tree to expand and contract. The result is splitting trunks and limbs, as well as breeding grounds for canker bores. Temperatures below minus 15 degrees Fahrenheit will kill even dormant buds.

Peaches also have to be thinned. While we have compounds (NAA) that will thin apples, no such product exists to remove peach blossoms or small peaches. You will find that removing small developing peaches is a time-consuming but necessary task—necessary because peach trees are heavy fruit setters. Nearly every blossom pollinates (sets) and becomes fruit. To leave them all on the tree would give you fully grown fruit the size of golf balls. Thinning also allows the tree to set new buds in August (in Michigan) for the next year. Too much fruit left on the tree will consume so much of the tree's energy that it will not set buds for the following year. If you don't thin, you'll be left with small, unsellable fruit one year and nothing the next.

Peach thinning is an expensive and time-consuming task. In 2002 we spent $5,000 to thin fifteen acres. Note that thinning is different from pruning. Pruning removes branches, which helps to shape the tree and ensures continued efficient production of fruit (new growth produces new buds). Thinning removes the already-formed fruit.

And as noted earlier, the sub-zero temps of 2014 and 2015 nearly wiped out our entire peach orchard. But I love peaches and we are replanting! Why? Because healthy, well-thinned peach trees will make money. Peaches are difficult to ship commercially because, in order to be shipped without damage, they must be picked while still quite firm. A firm peach is still green. If picked at this stage, it does not ripen properly or develop its full flavor. If, however, the peach is left on the tree until nearly ripe (still firm but with full color), it is one of the most luscious, succulent treats you can imagine. This will take some training of your customers. Most supermarket customers will tell you woeful stories of buying pithy peaches, with no taste even after they soften. But when they taste your tree-ripened fruit they'll be back for more.

All of this requires patience. You will also need a cold-storage facility to store the ripening fruit. Peaches will ripen very quickly in hot humid conditions. And since you are letting them stay on the tree longer, you must be prepared to get them picked and chilled quickly. Otherwise you risk losing them because, once they soften on the tree, they will fall and bruise.

It is for this reason that we take peaches to three or four city or county farmers' markets during July and August. Since our large traffic-flow months are September and October, we find it difficult to sell all our peach harvest at the orchard in August. Taking the fruit to the markets helps our summer cash flow and also allows us to advertise our products and encourage customers to come to the farm.

I consider peaches to be a ten- to twelve-year crop. This means we are always planting new trees to replace the ones that must be removed. You will find that in the northern climates you will lose between 10 and 20 percent of your peach trees each year, for reasons explained above. Many fruit growers have given up on peaches for this reason. But if you view the tree as having a relatively short life and you commit to raising good-quality tree-ripened fruit, you will make a profit on peaches.

Blueberries

We have two acres of this delicious, healthy fruit. They require minimum care and, in our climate, ripen in July, a good time for us. They need acidic soil: a pH of 5.5 or less. If you have these conditions, I recommend some acreage of blueberries.

I planted 1,800 blueberry bushes in 1980. We have three varieties, including Bluetta (an early-ripening berry), Bluecrop, and Jersey. In the last couple of years I have planted a hundred bushes of Elliots, a late-ripening variety. Blueberry bushes require much less care than any other fruit. Before 2010 I used no chemicals or fertilizer on the plants. Recently I have had to monitor the blueberry maggot and have used a mild insecticide to control the adult stage of this pest.

You will need protection from the birds as the fruit ripens. We cover about two acres with a bird-proof net and install a door to allow you-pick customers to enter the netted area. We remove the net after harvest and erect it again the following year. After two or three years the net must be replaced. We discovered some years ago that we need to remove the net annually because a heavy, wet snow will destroy the net and its supports. This happened to us twice in one year. The net was destroyed by a heavy winter storm; we replaced it in April, only to have a late snowstorm destroy it again! Overall, blueberries are a profitable and winning combination on any farm. Food and nutrition specialists extol the wonderful nutritional and medicinal qualities of this fruit.

In the past five years (2010–15), I have shipped three hundred blueberry bushes to Kenya in East Africa. I sent three different varieties that have been developed for more southern climates (they don't require the cooling hours that the northern varieties do). The varieties sent to Kenya were Misty Blue, Sharp Blue, and Biloxi Blue. These varieties only require 150 hours of cooling temperatures (32 degrees to 45 degrees) for dormancy, while Bluecrop requires over 700 hours of cooling. These varieties are being grown successfully in Florida and other areas in the southern United States. I have experimented with them in Kenya because there are no blueberries grown there and there would be a good market for local growers if we can get them to take. To date, I can only report marginal success. Most of the bushes flourish at the start, sending out a vigorous bloom and plentiful fruit. But then they seem to stagnate and refuse to grow. Only a few plants have taken and are showing growth. We plan to graft from these bushes and try to establish a new variety suitable to Kenya's climate.

Blueberries are a winner and have been very successful on our farm as a minor crop. They begin to mature in early July and last through most of August. This gives us a nice summer crop to supplement the peaches and plums. But test your soil first before planting: you must have a soil pH of 5.5 or less to grow them successfully.

Plums

Although the demand for plums is limited, I love growing and eating them. As with peaches, plums left on the tree to maturity will delight your customers. They are often picked unripe commercially and, like peaches, don't become sweet no matter how long you allow them to soften.

Plums require the same fertilizer and chemical control as peaches to prevent common problems like brown rot and plum curculio. They are thus easy to grow in combination with peaches. I have three varieties ripening at different times over a three- to four-week period in August—the same times as most of the peaches. I recommend three varieties: Simka, Methly, and Byron Gold.

Other fruit

We have grown pears and apricots in the past. But I have found that it is easier and more profitable to purchase these fruits than to grow them. When in season, they are relatively inexpensive to buy and resell. Pears ripen at the wrong time for us, between peaches and apples. The demand is not very strong, nor is it long lasting. The same is true for apricots.

I hasten to add that conditions may be different in your area and you will want to examine this before you plant. For example, I know of several farms in the eastern states that do very well with both sweet and sour cherries. It's an excellent money-maker, with the fruit ripening early in the summer.

Although strawberries are extremely important to many you-pick operations, I don't like growing them, for three reasons:

1. They require a high concentration of chemicals to control weeds, fungus, and insects.
2. The pick-your-own crowd is steadily diminishing. Fewer and fewer people have time to pick.
3. Our season is very short: about three weeks. If you have unusually hot or wet conditions during this time, you lose a significant portion of your crop.

If you are going to California or the South, where there are longer growing conditions, you may want to consider this crop. It is a very popular item. If you are in the North, however, the opposite applies.

Pumpkins

We plant eight to ten acres of pumpkins. We mix the varieties to include the regular fifteen to twenty-five pounders and the smaller "pie" size (three to six pounds). We also include a few of the extra-large size. Pumpkins provide additional income and activities for our you-pick customers in late September and October. In fact, in October, pumpkins draw more customers than apples.

Pumpkins are relatively easy to germinate and grow. Powdery mildew became a problem in the last decade (2001–2010), but to avoid the weekly spraying that most commercial growers do, I plant early—around the last week in May in Michigan—and the fruit is nearly mature when powdery mildew strikes in mid-August. While most of the leaves are affected by the mildew, the pumpkin matures and develops color in spite of loss of leaves.

While I don't get the yield and size that commercial growers do, I avoid the expense and heavy use of chemicals. I purchase several hundred tons to supplement the pumpkins we grow. Though competitive with scores of pumpkin-producing farms nearby, we make money from our pumpkin patches.

We sell pumpkins by the pound: 39 cents per pound in 2015. It is time-consuming on busy October weekends to weigh each pumpkin, but I feel it gives us the best return per unit. No small farm should be without this crop. October revenues represent about 50 to 60 percent of our total revenues for the year, and pumpkins represent about 25 percent of that total. Customers love this crop.

Sunflowers, Indian corn, and popcorn

These crops generate interest but little return. We plant an acre of the above and open the field for "pick-your-own." We plant the sunflowers the first week of July so they bloom in mid-September. They make a great photo opportunity when in bloom and we sell a few heads for the seeds. We stop at the popcorn field for the school field trips. Many students and teachers presume popcorn comes in a bag to be popped in a microwave. They are surprised to see that it grows on a cob like sweet corn! I often give an ear of popcorn to each participant in small groups in addition to their apples. For larger groups of twenty students or more I present three or four ears to the teacher to demonstrate to their students. Indian corn is always popular, but it is easier to buy and resell.

In conclusion, I recommend limiting your acreage of apples. Most commercial orchards today are opting for very concentrated plantings of apple trees at spacing of 4' x 8' with up to a thousand trees per acre. If you plant this way I would limit planting to ten acres or less. Apples are readily available to purchase to supplement your production.

Peaches are still winners, even with the threat of damage (as we experienced in 2014–15). My previous loss of a peach crop was in 1994 and then again in 2014. Hence, I had twenty years of successful harvests. Blueberries are also a great money earner if your soil conditions are right. If you don't have the proper pH (5.5), don't plant them.

Pumpkins are also a winner. No successful farm market can be without them, and if you allow customers into your fields it is an added attraction.

While there are some hugely successful strawberry and cherry farms in Michigan (and elsewhere in the Midwest), I would minimize the planting of these fruits, as well as plums, pears, and apricots.

Chapter 7
Observations about Retail Sales

In addition to growing fruit, we are also in retail sales. Our store encompasses four thousand square feet of sales area, including a donut kitchen and cider-making room. On busy weekends in September and October we bake pies, donuts, and other baked goods.

I have learned that successful sales are contingent on four areas: advertising, displays, customers, and pricing.

Advertising
After thirty-six years of growing and selling fruit, I still don't know the most effective way to advertise. I have used most media, including radio, TV, newspapers, billboards, and the Internet. I believe in advertising, and spend 4 to 6 percent of our annual budget on it. We are closed for nearly seven months during the year and to get customers back when we open, I have to advertise. We advertise in six ways, as described below.

We begin by placing small retail ads in three local papers: the *Toledo Blade*, the *Monroe Evening News*, and South Detroit's *News-Herald*. The ad is surrounded by an apple design; I use the same design all year. The copy for the ad is changed weekly, depending on what is ripe and what activity we are presenting. While the Internet is becoming the primary source of news for most young customers, the newspaper remains an effective tool for me.

We have often used radio ads for special weekend activities like the antique car show and kids' weekends. These ads, though more expensive than the newspaper, have given us a boost for our important weekends. But I am dubious of their ultimate value. You reach a very limited audience, depending on the station, and to get the peak listening times, like the morning and evening drive times, you pay a premium. In 2009 I stopped running these radio ads.

Television advertising is beyond my budget except for unusual circumstances. Several years ago, the Lyon's department store in Toledo, Ohio, wanted to do a fall advertising campaign using the orchard as a backdrop. They took miles of film footage and used only a fraction. I obtained some excess footage and used it for some TV ads, avoiding the production costs. More effectively, I have invited local TV news anchors to come to the orchard for a story. We often have something of interest for them. For example, an unusual pumpkin crop, blueberries that can be picked under a giant net, or apples that were affected by a spring frost. You will find that news people are hungry for news, especially something unusual or weather related.

School field trips have contributed to our advertising efforts. As mentioned earlier, we send home a flyer with each participant, and on weekends often see children who have been on a recent field trip and are returning with their parents. While we now have fewer field-trip participants, this is still an important part of our advertising efforts.

The Internet is a vital source of advertising, and we provide information through our website, Twitter, and Facebook. My college-age employees created our Facebook and Twitter accounts. Since our target audience is twenty- and thirty-year-olds with young children, social networking is important. Directions, prices, hours, events, and personal information about the orchard are all accessible on the website: erieorchards.com. Our field trips and craft booths can be booked directly on the website. Over 50 percent of our field trips now book through the website.

In 2014 and 2015 our Facebook page has become a major part of our outreach. We are receiving several thousand "hits" each week. Satisfied Facebook users who display pictures of their visit expand our exposure geometrically. Employees Zander Stuart and Bobbi Cadaret provide daily updates outlining our current activities. As a result our newspaper advertising budget has been slashed. If other small companies have reduced their newspaper ad budgets as we have, it harbors bad news for printed newspapers!

Satisfied customers, without question, are our best source of advertising. Every person coming to our orchard is a potential advertiser, who will spread the word to family and friends. During our weekly meetings with employees I repeatedly emphasize the importance of good customer relations. A friendly greeting, a willingness to help if needed, and a thank you with each purchase are essential for customer satisfaction.

Displays

Americans love the big and bold: big pickup trucks, big homes, and big stores with big displays. Have you ever been in a store that has only partially filled shelves (one row of goods with nothing behind)? Chances are, that store will be gone next time you visit. As customers, we want lots of produce on display, we want the shelves full, and we want it all clean and neat.

While I can never compete with the huge produce sections of a Kroger supermarket or produce markets, I can have our retail store packed with apples, jams, jellies, and gift items. Our pumpkin displays are huge, as I often purchase several semi loads to get us going in the fall.

Our displays at the farmers' markets illustrate the above. When we're selling from a full table loaded with fresh blueberries, peaches, and summer apples, the selling is fast and furious. As our supply decreases during the late morning and our table is less than full, it may take an hour or more to finish selling the same product. To the average customer, it looks like we're going out of business and our display is not as attractive.

On busy fall weekends I have two or three employees constantly restocking our apple displays, the cider cooler, and other shelves. We don't want to appear to be out of stock!

The popularity of "box" stores (Lowe's, Home Depot, Menards, etc.) demonstrates conclusively that big and bold sells. So, no matter how small your sales area, stock to the ceiling with your goods.

Pricing your product

I believe in high prices. A few years ago I tried to match prices from other competitors. I realized that, regardless of how low I went, someone would always complain that the price was too high. So I have decided to rely on quality and keep the price higher than the competition. Here are a few thoughts on pricing:

1. If you are going to be the highest price in town, you have to have the best quality, or at least the perception of the best quality. Our cider is the highest priced of any cider in the metro Toledo area. We are consistently 30 to 49 percent higher than anyone else. And yet I always sell all the cider that I budgeted for the year. We take great pride in mixing the apples to get a blend that combines both tart and

sweet apples. We let customers know that we use fewer chemicals and use only surface insecticides and not the systemic, which can leave a residue in the apples and juice. We make the cider daily in front of a large window where customers can watch the entire process. Most of the cider purchased has been made within the previous twenty-four hours. We also process the cider through a UV filtering system that acts as a pasteurizing agent, but that does not heat the cider and alter the flavor.

If this formula works, why not lower the price and sell larger quantities? Because I can make less cider at a reduced cost (fewer apples, less labor, fewer jugs and supplies) and still get the revenue I need to ensure a healthy profit. The profit is in the price, and the higher my price the better my profit.

2. We have some products that have an inelastic demand as related to price. By raising the price we may see some loss of demand for the product, but not nearly as much as might be expected. For example, by raising the price of our home-baked pies from $10.95 in 2009 to $12.95 in 2010 (nearly a 20 percent increase), we assumed there would be a 20 percent decline in the two thousand pies we were selling annually. However, we experienced no noticeable decline at all. The pies are baked in our own ovens and we are constantly baking during the day, generating smells that are hard to resist. We experienced the same result when we raised the price of our apple

fritters. For example, we raised apple fritters from $3.50 each to $4.50 each from 2013 to 2015 with no noticeable reduction in demand.

3. I believe passionately in my product. We ensure it is fresh, and constantly monitor the quality. And I believe if you have a passion for your product, you can and should sell it at a higher price. Even at the farmers' markets that we attend in the summer months, where the competition is very keen, I make sure our prices are slightly higher than the others. We compensate by giving out free samples of our products. It is hard to resist buying a tree-ripened peach in the middle of the summer when you have tried a fresh sample.

Although we get some complaining about our "high" prices, I believe the higher prices, along with good customer service, have done more than any other factor in contributing to the success of our business. You can't satisfy everyone! See the following pages for total expenses and net income for the years 1986–2015.

We are always experimenting with new products. We tried serving ice cream but found it unsuccessful; the same was true for homemade fudge. We also started a gift shop, but that was much too competitive and seasonal for us. We now rent space for a gift shop.

We have built enormous success with some key products, including apple and pumpkin butter, apple fritters and our homemade donuts. Home-baked pies sell well on fall weekends.

Although our net income remained fairly consistent after peaking in 2003, it rose sharply again in 2014 and 2015. Total expenses remained relatively consistent from 2003 through 2015. Some of this is a result of lower interest expense (see interest chart on p. 14).

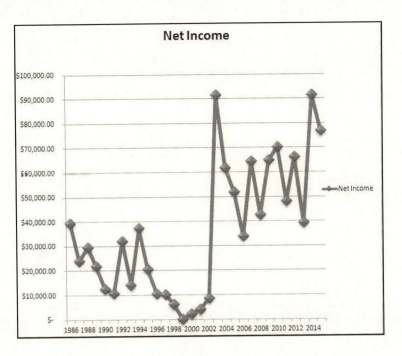

1986- $39,377.00	1987- $24,012.00	1988- $29,462.00
1989- $21,708.00	1990- $12,576.00	1991- $10,738.00
1992- $32,003	1993- $14,058	1994- $37,121.00
1995- $20,330.00	1996- $10,418.00	1997- $10,180.00
1998- $6,155.00	1999- $40.00	2000- $2,083.00
2001- $4,023.00	2002- $8,444.00	2003- $91,391.00
2004- $61,621.00	2005- $51,796.00	2006- $33,834.00
2007- $64,357.00	2008- $42,595.00	2009- $64,949.00
2010- $70,182.00	2011- $48,136.00	2012- $66,248.00
2013- $39,250.00	2014- $91,434.00	2015- $76,745.00

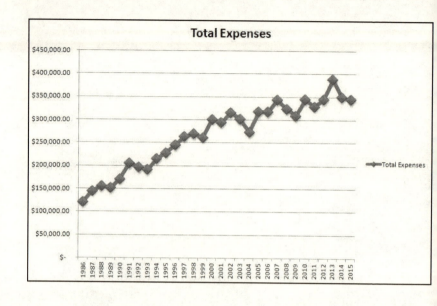

1986- $120,587.61	1987- $144,545.09	1988- $155,158.00
1989- $151,633.00	1990- $170,547.00	1991- $204,523.00
1992- $196,551.00	1993- $191,180.00	1994- $214,218.00
1995- $227,590.00	1996- $244,561.00	1997- $262,832.00
1998- $269,349.00	1999- $261,134.00	2000- $300,803.00
2001- $294,272.00	2002- $315,716.00	2003- $301,486.00
2004- $273,339.00	2005- $317,201.00	2006- $317,908.00
2007- $343,963.00	2008- $324,220.00	2009- $309,396.00
2010- $344,530.00	2011- $329,363.00	2012- $344,424.00
2013- $388,369.00	2014- $349,404.00	2015- $345,058.00

Note: The low net income levels in 1999, 2000, and 2001 can be partially explained by very high depreciation expenses. We made several capital purchases, including equipment, trees, and new buildings. This contributed to high depreciation expense and low net income. See depreciation chart on p. 20.

Chapter 8
Customer and Employee Relations

We hire forty to fifty part-time employees each year. Some are regular and have been with us for thirty years or longer. But many come for a year or two and need training. My first question to a prospective employee is: "Why would you come to Erie Orchards and Cider Mill, when you can buy the same product at all the chain grocery stores or large produce markets?" Many answer that they would come because our fruit is fresher and it is good to buy locally. But I also want to hear that our place is a friendly and helpful place to shop.

I emphasize to each prospective employee the importance of a smile and greeting. We don't have to hover over our customers, but if the customer has a question we are there to give answers. A pleasant and informative greeting on the phone is vital.

I love working in our retail store on the busiest weekends, handing out donuts or bagging at the registers. But mostly my work is in the orchard or office. Thus, I need employees who will represent me and our family. Employees are a crucial element: they can make or break your name and reputation.

I insist on a weekly meeting with my store and field employees. I ask each one to give an accounting of their work and if they have any problems or suggestions. These meetings are often short, with a brief description of events for the next weekend. I encourage and praise employees often. And I strongly urge them to share ideas with the group. This is not easy for new employees, who may be insecure and shy, but once they open up, it can be a healthy and helpful exchange.

Like advertising, knowing how to get the best bang for your buck in hiring employees is not easy. Bright and enthusiastic interviews do not always translate into good employees. Here are some factors I consider:

- I look for someone who may be a regular to our orchard as a customer and who has a love for the place and feels it would be great place to work.
- I look for individuals who are not looking for full-time work but are interested in supplementing household income, saving for Christmas, their children's education, etc. I also ask that each employee commit to staying with us through the harvest months of September and October.
- I look for confidence, an easy smile, and honesty.

- I look for individuals who live nearby and don't have transportation issues.
- I look for individuals who respond positively when asked if they will stay to help clean the store after hours (mopping the floors, cleaning the bathroom and kitchens).
- I observe their dress, neatness, and willingness to greet me with a firm handshake and smile.

Even with those guidelines, hiring is often a gamble. Roughly one in three of our new employees leaves before the season ends or has issues that we can't live with. Our young high schoolers are hired in the summer and make a promise to work on fall weekends. Then come homecoming, school functions, church outings, etc., and we lose them at our most critical times.

With three to five thousand visitors to our farm every weekend, it is imperative that we have a full staff to serve the customers. And it is terribly frustrating when employees we hired in the summer—when we did not need them—don't show up when needed. But it happens.

While I am generous with praise to our employees, I have rules: no cell phone use (including texting) in front of customers, no smoking on the premises, and absolutely no rude or disrespectful remarks to customers. I have let teens go because of their inability to be without their cell phones. I have not rehired those suspected of theft. I have also learned not to implicate anyone when theft occurs. Usually the truth emerges, but to threaten all or question all is very unsettling to the majority who are honest. My experience confirms that a quiet and reflective approach is usually most effective. Employees often come forward and confirm what I have already suspected.

Though the hiring experience is challenging, I have also had some jewels. Young people who can learn the cash register in minutes. Women who haven't been employed in years, but make an extraordinary effort. Young men who have learned to safely drive the tractors and equipment and become incredibly helpful. And older, reliable employees who return each year and faithfully fulfill their tasks.

I've made many lasting friends. Though I don't socialize regularly with most employees, I have several who are lifelong friends. To counterbalance the few who disappoint, there will be many others whose determination, loyalty, and hard work will astound you.

Here are a few of the employees who have contributed to our success:

Ron Cousino worked for us during the late 1970s and early '80s and became an excellent worker both in the farm and in our market. With our encouragement, he graduated from Michigan State University and now works for the US Forest Service. Gary Martin and Harlan Leutz were indispensible orchard workers during the 1980s. Mark Putman was for many years our orchard manager and worked our Detroit and Ann Arbor farmers' markets in the 1990s. Lisa Holt introduced many innovative and fresh ideas while managing our store in 2000 to 2003. And Natalie Sargent (Kirby) worked as a high school student and later became store manager in 2004. Her youthful outlook and computer skills helped modernize our cash registers and accounting. Caitlin Kreamer began as a high school student in 2011 and helped edit two books published by Steve: the present volume, *Farming and Flourishing on Sixty Acres*, and *Letters from Northern Kenya: A Young American Couple's Journey, 1974–1977*. All of the above employees have moved on to other jobs or universities but some come back to help on busy weekends.

Currently, Valerie and Mike Mitchell manage the store and orchard, respectively. They have made our net income grow to new levels over the last five years, 2010 to 2015.

Bobbi Cadaret, who books all our school tours and crafters, and keeps our website current, is indispensable in our modern connected world. Randall and Nancy Gammon (both deceased in 2014), Lorna and Larry Eddings, and Mary Jane and Bryon Gartee have all worked for us for more than thirty years. Without their faithful service and enormous contributions, we would not be here.

Chapter 9
New Equipment and Capital Investments

"There are two kinds of fools, equally dangerous: Those who think everything is good because it is new and those who think nothing is good that is not old."
—A. C. Trench

In business, as in life, maintaining a balance is vitally important. For the first twenty years of our business I used secondhand (and third-hand) trucks, tractors, forklifts, and most other equipment. Over time, I updated our equipment as needed. A few essential pieces I purchased new very early. For example, I purchased a new orchard sprayer within the first couple years. The last problem I wanted was to be tinkering with an old chemical sprayer when I needed to be in the orchard spraying for disease or pests. Today I have a new sprayer on standby. I consider this an absolute necessity, because when a disease or pest enters the orchard, you sometimes have a very short window in which to control it.

By contrast, I used older trucks and tractors for most of my business career. In 2007, when my mother passed on and left a small inheritance, I purchased a new cube truck for hauling our produce to markets. It was the first large truck we had purchased new in thirty years. More recently, I have taken advantage of corporate tax benefits and purchased several new tractors (usually one a year) over the last eight to ten years.

I am a believer in the philosophy of the prodigious accumulator of wealth (PAW) as described in *The Millionaire Next Door* by Thomas J. Stanley and William D. Danko. Stanley and Danko assert that the small businessman down your street who has a modest house, used vehicles, and a wife who still shops with coupons is probably much wealthier (a PAW) than his counterparts living in the best neighborhoods, with the best cars and best clothes—they are UAWs (under accumulators of wealth). In other words, the person who watches what he buys, is not concerned about outward personal appearances, and generally lives modestly is going to create wealth much faster than the "conspicuous" consumer. Although one has to wade through lots of statistics, this book is a must read for anyone starting a business.

Buying equipment and making significant capital purchases require some thought and careful evaluation. Ask yourself the following questions:

- Is the new equipment absolutely essential for running the business efficiently?
- Can I see increased revenues immediately with any new purchase?
- Do I have the cash flow to pay if financed?
- Is the maintenance of the existing equipment so high that I can justify the new purchase to cut these high costs?

I admit that I'm a sucker for shiny new equipment that works well. But I also understand that it does not always justify the cost. For example, I have used an old corn planter purchased for $250 for nearly twenty years to plant about thirty rows of Indian corn and popcorn every year. I use the planter for about half an hour a year. After several years of dealing with leaking fertilizer hoppers, uneven seed distribution, and rusty chains and pulleys, I purchased a new planter for $8,000 in 2011. It works great, but I quickly realized I could have easily opted for another used planter at a fraction of the cost. Frustration got the best of me on that purchase.

In 2014 we switched from older cash registers to iPads. We now have ten of them, operating at each of our sales areas, including ticket sales, the bakery, and the you-pick barn. Using the iPads along with Square (the mobile-payment company) gives us an efficient method to record and track all transactions. It also allows for fast credit-card processing. I am convinced that staying up to date on the technology of paying for merchandise is important.

I spend a couple months in East Africa each winter. A pioneering cell phone payment system, M-Pesa, is thriving in Kenya and Tanzania. In 2015, 20 percent of all transactions in Kenya were done using the cell phone. They have evolved faster there than in the United States because of the prepaid credit system. The phone credits have become marketable commodities used for buying goods, paying utility bills, and even paying for hotel accommodations. This fast, convenient system will soon come to us. Those of us in the retail trade must be prepared to accept mobile phone payments—something we plan to do in 2016.

Chapter 10
Customer Relations

Richard Branson, founder of the Virgin Group, writes a column on business life that I often find helpful. In a column in the Feb. 21, 2012 issue of Kenya's *Daily Nation*, he described a decision to save money by halting the free distribution of ice cream bars on Virgin Atlantic flights. Soon after stopping this practice he received an uproar of protests, with customers writing in to tell him that it was the little touches like the ice cream bars that set his airline apart. Branson reintroduced them immediately.

I am going to summarize four basic principles of customer relations that a former employee, Jim Brien, developed as he worked for me and that he shares in the business class we teach together.

Being pleasant and cordial
I insist that every customer who enters our retail store and orchard is met with a friendly greeting. Our parking attendants are often the first people encountered at our establishment. I encourage them to greet customers with a smile. And I insist that we

will answer all questions about our product and assist the customer in any way possible. Nothing annoys me more than an inattentive salesperson or one who fails to make even a perfunctory greeting. As mentioned above, I teach a customer-relations course to prospective business owners in Toledo, Ohio. When I share the above, it is always acknowledged that a pleasant greeting is essential to a good shopping experience and reason to return to that establishment.

Over the past few months, I have been looking for a new or used pickup truck. I returned to a small, locally owned dealership where I'd had a positive buying experience in the past. This time, unfortunately, the salesman repeatedly ignored my phone calls and did not respond to my inquiries. I often take several weeks to decide on a vehicle purchase. Because of his inattentiveness, in spite of my previous positive experience, I am going elsewhere. Good service is not a one-time option!

Friends often ask why I go to East Africa for the winter months when my orchard is closed. Aside from my experimental blueberry planting, I go because of the consistently friendly people I encounter. They draw me back yearly and I always look forward to their friendly faces and smiles.

Fairness

Nothing will alienate your customers faster than unfair treatment. We will, for example, refund or exchange any item purchased—without question. We often have some cider returns, especially in early September, when temperatures can reach the eighties. If you place your fresh cider in a locked trunk or car in extreme heat, the cider rapidly hardens and develops a vinegary taste. We know this occurs and we know it is not our fault, but we exchange it anyway.

Whether a customer is genuinely shortchanged or simply claims that this is the case, we will cover the difference. In short, we will honor any dispute in the customer's favor. We discuss these problems later to avoid them in the future. But we always err on the side of the customer.

Recently, a customer called for a bushel of Honeycrisp apples and one of our salespersons mistakenly quoted our regular apple bushel price of $40. However, due to the high cost of Honeycrisp apples and the fact that we have a very limited supply, we don't sell the Honeycrisp by the bushel. We sell only in small quantities or by the pound. In 2012, the Honeycrisp cost $45 per bushel wholesale. The customer knew this was a mistake by our salesperson but insisted on buying at the quoted price. I complied, even though the customer used this obvious mistake to his advantage.

Of course, there are instances when a customer will try to claim falsely that our price was quoted wrongly and we will not comply. But this happens very infrequently. Over the years we have developed an atmosphere of fairness and I know it has benefited our sales. And fairness begets an added benefit with the employees. They know we run an honest company and that leads to sense of pride working for us.

Availability

Most customers shop for some need. We can't match the prices of the large grocery stores and produce markets, but we can beat them on our customer service. We are available to answer your questions about fruit. How many apples to make a pie? Which varieties are best for cooking? When is the best time to pick and buy peaches and blueberries? How long will a pumpkin last? What apples are used to make cider? We have the answers and are available.

In the business startup class I teach at the Assets Toledo nonprofit agency, I ask: What is the biggest disappointment customers have when going shopping? I offer four possible answers:

1. Rude salespeople
2. Can't find anyone to help
3. Not having in stock what you advertised
4. Long checkout lines

Most students answer No. 2 (can't find anyone to help). Being available and having staff aware of this is critical to your success in small business.

Get connected

My store manager, Valerie Mitchell, breeds dogs. Over the years she has posted pictures of her new puppies on our bulletin board. Dog-loving customers often chat with Valerie about their dogs and ask how her puppies are doing. This small gesture has allowed Valerie to connect with scores of our customers.

Occasionally I recognize a customer, and will make a special effort to greet him or her. If I know they have come to pick fruit, I will sometimes drive into the orchard and show them the best location for picking that day. I have made a connection with that customer.

Many customers come only once or twice a year and greet me on their annual visit. I often inquire about their children, as I have watched many of their children grow to adults with children now of their own. I have made a connection with them.

At times my connection may simply be a casual nod of recognition to a customer I do not know but who has previously visited. Nevertheless, that nod is a gesture of appreciation for their business—it is a symbol of our connection.

Customers love and crave recognition. Recently, while walking the crowded streets of Nairobi, a cell phone repairman with whom I had worked spotted me and crossed a busy street to greet me. He connected with me, and because of this I will continue to use him to service my cell phone.

Summary

As my friend, Jim Brien, says in a class we jointly teach: "The difference between a hobby and a business is the customer and making the sale." Without customers you are not in business; and without satisfied customers you are not in business for long.

Four basic principles drive our customer relations: Being pleasant and polite, being fair, being available, and finally, getting connected.

Remember these!

Chapter 11
Conclusion

Remember the three major decisions in buying your farm:

The first factor is size and location. Stay as close to a metropolitan area as possible. When considering your purchase, draw a circle with a radius of thirty miles around your farm. You should have a minimum of 500,000 people living within that circle. This guarantees adequate traffic flow. Every successful retailer will tell you the importance of adequate traffic flow.

The size of your farm may vary, but you need sufficient acreage to give the impression of a thriving, productive farm. In my opinion, twenty to thirty acres is small, while eighty to a hundred is large. Our sixty-two acres give the impression of a large farm. There is adequate room for several hundred people to come, harvest, and enjoy the open space. Yet it is not so large as to be unwieldy to mow and maintain.

Buy low and work creatively to finance the farm with the best interest rates possible. Don't forget to explore the United States Department of Agriculture

(USDA) guaranteed loan programs for farmers. Also explore rates and terms with Greenstone Farm Credit Services, which specializes in farm loans.

Second, focus your entire vision on retail. You may be tempted to sell some of your crop wholesale—to chain stores or large orchard operations that will package and sell your fruit. Don't do it! Strive to grow and sell your product to the end user—the retail customer.

If you decide to purchase with a partner, choose him or her carefully. A marriage can be dissolved and your life will go on. Dissolve a partnership and you may lose your livelihood. My partnership functioned successfully but, after our goals differed, we agreed to split. It was amicable, but not all partnerships end pleasantly. Be cautious.

Finally, avoid disabling debt if possible. Review your projected income and expenses and then reduce projected income by 10 percent and increase projected costs by 25 percent. If you can still handle the debt, you have a good starting point.

Maintain some other income if possible. As described, my wife worked as a social worker for a local hospital. Her income and health insurance "saved" us during the lean years.

Here is a quick summary of some of the other key areas mentioned in the book. As described by Charles J. Givens in *Wealth Without Risk*, your biggest lifetime expense will be income taxes. The farm will soften this blow if you choose wisely.

Talk to several accountants before you decide how to establish your business as a partnership, sole proprietor, or corporation. And remember the importance of depreciation.

Though very competitive, school field trips are essential for those slow weekdays. It will take prodding to get teachers to bring their classes but it's worth your effort. Preschools, daycare centers, and senior housing facilities are good prospects and seem to have fewer transportation and financial issues. Seniors pose some extra challenges, but we have two wagons with wheelchair access. To my knowledge we are the only orchard to offer wheelchair access and have benefited by hosting nearly all the senior housing field trips in our area.

The essence of your operation must be entertainment. I described six weekends that generate up to 70 percent of our total income. The majority of our customers come on weekends and a typical family will purchase cider and donuts, along with a pony and/or hayride and a visit to our corn maze. They may not even purchase fruit. While the apple orchard and pumpkin patches may be an attraction to help bring customers to your farm, the income from your entertainment will soon eclipse that from your fruit.

Selecting and planting your fruit crops will require some careful planning. Peaches, though difficult to maintain in northern climates, produce fruit faster than most other tree fruits. In Michigan we harvest some peaches in the third year after planting.

Apples require four to five years to give any significant production.

When planting apples you must consider the varieties that are popular for your area. Don't be tempted by the nursery catalogs or apple consultants to plant the newest "fad" variety. Include some of traditional varieties that are popular in your area. For example, Golden Delicious, Jonagold, Granny Smiths, and Jonathans are the most popular you-pick varieties for us. We have planted Fuji, Braeburn, and Honeycrisp, but we still like the traditional varieties listed above.

Pumpkins will bring a healthy profit. They also attract customers when the demand for apples wanes in late October. We plant several varieties, ranging in size from the very small two- or three-pounders to the giant hundred-pounders. However, by far the biggest demand is for the twenty- to thirty-pounders.

Properly pricing your products will influence your profits. When I teach a class on entrepreneurship, many students suggest they want to sell a good product at the lowest possible price. To me, this suggests a lack of confidence in your product and your ability to sell it. If you are pricing below your competition, you will always struggle with customers who want an even lower price. Price your product higher than the competition, then work diligently on quality and salesmanship. Remember: low prices mean low profits for those of us in small enterprises.

Hiring the reliable, pleasant, and trustworthy

employee requires a great deal of effort. Identify some variables you want in each employee and use these in your interview. For example, does your prospective employee have transportation? Do they have knowledge of your place as a customer? Are their outside interests going to conflict with your weekend needs—cheerleading, football games, homecoming, etc. For our retail help, I look for a quick learner on the cash register who is fast and efficient. They must have an easy smile and be able to engage with the customer. And they must also work well with all the employees. For those working in the orchard, I look for people who are careful with the machinery and see jobs that need to be done without asking. I will hire most employees who are field workers with this condition: that we will evaluate their performance after a week of work and make a mutual decision to continue or not.

Buying the newest and most sophisticated equipment when starting may impress your friends and competitors but it won't help your bank account. I have searched for and purchased used equipment for most of my career. Only in the last ten years have I updated our most important equipment, including tractors, forklifts, donut makers, and cash registers.

A few years ago, a farmer acquaintance of mine decided to enter the produce business. The price of corn and soybeans (his main crops) dropped and he decided to convert some acreage to fruits and vegetables, including sweet corn, peppers, melons, and tomatoes. He built and equipped an entire new building with all the latest washing, grading, and packaging equipment to market the produce. One year later he auctioned the entire lot at a considerable loss. Beware of going too far too fast!

I spend several hours teaching and promoting to my employees the four essential points of customer relations: Being cordial and pleasant, fairness, availability, and getting connected. Use them with your customers.

My attitude toward my customers and philosophy of selling fruit has rewarded me with forty years of successfully growing a business. In spite of severe weather, loss of crops, disgruntled employees, onerous government regulations, and all the other problems facing a small business, I believe that adhering to these fundamental principles will make your business successful.

Although I am nearing "retirement" age, I am embarking on a new enterprise of planting blueberries and developing small-scale farming in Kenya and Tanzania. And I will continue to operate the orchard for the foreseeable future. It's impossible for me to give up the daily stimulation of running a business with its many challenges and rewards.

I hope these reflections help you in your pursuit of your passion.

Notes

Assets Toledo is a nonprofit agency developed by the Mennonite Church's Economic Development Association (MEDA). It is committed to helping individuals start their business by providing a thirteen-week course on how to set up and successfully operate a business. Various business leaders, attorneys, and accountants volunteer their time and teach a session. The Assets Toledo program began in 2001 and has successfully graduated more than 1,700 students.

I want to give credit to Nancy, my wife of forty-six years. She has been a great source of encouragement and support through all the forty years. She has been a social worker for Toledo and Flower Hospital in Toledo, Ohio, for more than thirty years. Her salary and benefits contributed to our success, especially in the "lean" years.

References

Tobias, Andrew P. *The Only Investment Guide You'll Ever Need*. Orlando: Harcourt, Inc., 2005.

Givens, Charles J. *Wealth Without Risk: How to Develop a Personal Fortune without Going Out on a Limb*. New York: Simon and Schuster, 1988.

Trump, Donald, and Tony Schwartz. *Trump: The Art of the Deal*. New York: Random House, 1988.

Stanley, Thomas J., and William D. Danko. *The Millionaire Next Door: The Surprising Secrets of America's Wealthy*. Atlanta, GA: Longstreet Press, 1996.

About the Author

Steve Elzinga has spent forty years raising and selling fruit in Michigan. He has a BA in Economics from Michigan State University and an MA in Economics from Wayne State University in Detroit. He and his wife, Nancy, have three grown children, Marna, Jesse, and Elise, and four grandchildren. They live in Lambertville, Michigan, and Nairobi, Kenya.